Great Gadgets

Contents

Great Gadgets

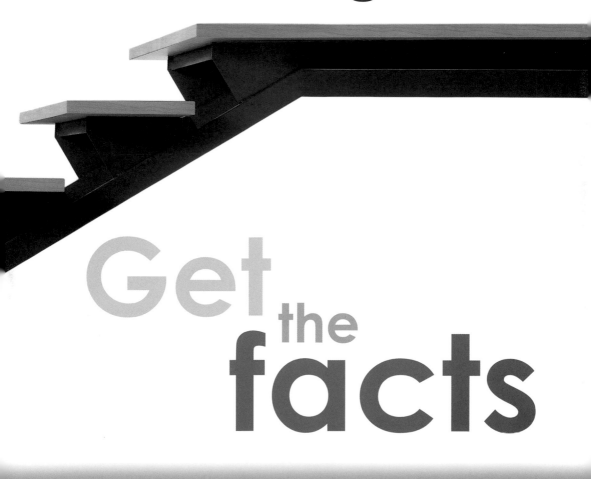

Get the facts

Great gadgets

This gadget was invented around 2,000 years ago by a man called **Hero**.

The **fire** made **steam** in the big pot. The steam went into the round ball, and came out of the nozzles. This made the ball spin round and round.

It's great fun, but what use is it?

Hero had invented the **steam engine**.

1 Kg

1 Kg

In 1882, someone invented a gadget to **wake you up** in the morning.

Instead of ringing a bell, it kept **dropping weights** on your head until you woke up.

That's the **problem** with inventions.

Sometimes they get invented before anybody can think what to do with them. Sometimes, they are just – **useless**!

Here are some **really useful inventions** from the past. Why do you think they were so important?

A needle made of bone.

A book.

A plough.

A spear head made of metal.

A T.V. remote.

A wheel.

A stone axe.

7

Entertainment

Some of our favourite gadgets are for playing music.

1

Can you put these music players on a time line?

2

Videos
Photos
Podcasts
Extras
Settings
Shuffle Songs

MENU

3

4

5

6

7

The answers are on the last page of the book.

Keeping in touch

So how does a **mobile phone** work?

A mobile phone is really a **radio** that sends and receives messages.

The country is divided up into small areas called **cells**. Each cell has a **radio transmitter**.

When you go from one cell to another, your phone sends a **message**. This message is sent through a cable to a **computer**.

The **computer** now knows where you are, so it can send your **phone calls** and **text messages** to the **right transmitter**.

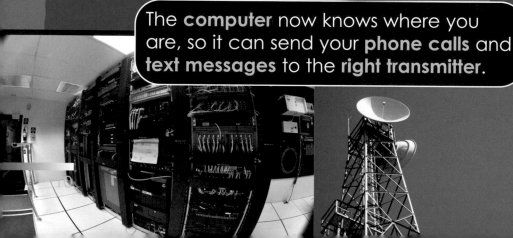

How do emails know which computer to go to?

An **email message** needs **extra information** to make sure it goes to the right place.

The address of the **mail server** of the person you are sending the message to.

What's a mail server?

A computer that stores messages and sends them out to the right person. This will belong to the company that provides your Internet (your **ISP**).

The name of the person you are sending the message to.

So for **whizzkid@ransominternet.com** – **ransominternet.com** is the mail server and **whizzkid** is the name of the person you are sending the message to.

Someone's tracking you ...

Some people who have committed crimes are tagged instead of being locked up.

The tag is worn round their ankle. It sends out a message like a mobile phone. This means the police can keep track of the person wherever they go.

Robots

People used to think robots would look something like this:

Or even like this ...

In fact, they are more likely to look like this:

Robots can do jobs that are too dangerous for people to do, like defusing a bomb.

A *bombot*, used to defuse bombs.

A good house-cleaning robot would need to be able to:

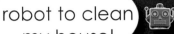 I want a robot to clean my house!

 But would it work?

 move around without bumping into things or getting stuck in corners.

 climb stairs (at least as well as a Dalek!)

know the **difference** between **rubbish** on the floor and **important things** like money or keys.

Some engineers are going back to an old idea – making robots that look like people.

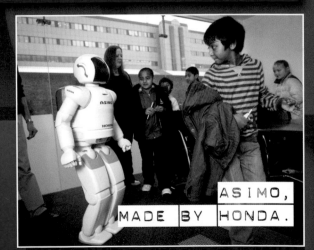

ASIMO, MADE BY HONDA.

Scientists say in the future computers could be more intelligent than people.

You want me to do **what**?

But that might be a problem ...

Computers

Here are some amazingly wrong predictions about computers.

 In 1943 the chairman of IBM said that he thought the world would only need **five computers**.

 In 1977 someone said there was **no reason** why anyone would want a **computer** in their **home**.

 In 1949 someone thought that computers of the future would weigh as little as **one and a half tons**.

 In 1981 Bill Gates said **640kB** of **memory** should be **enough** for anybody.

Most people think computers look like this:

But often computers are part of something else, like a **car** or **washing machine** or an **MP3 player**. These are called **embedded computers**.

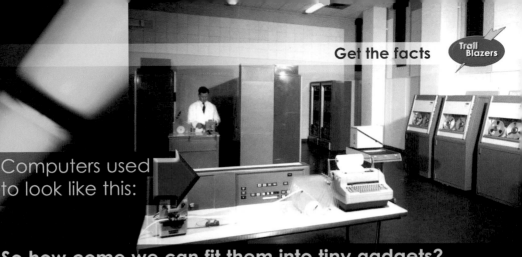

Computers used to look like this:

So how come we can fit them into tiny gadgets?

Because of **microchips**. A microchip can shrink down all the parts you need on to a tiny chip, smaller than a finger nail.

Will they get any smaller?

Probably. Scientists are building **quantum computers**, made from parts the size of atoms!

Virtual worlds

Life getting boring? You can now use your **computer** to live in a **virtual world**! You can be who you like, make friends, even go to school!

The virtual reality helmets of the future will make it seem just like real life!

But what would happen if you forget who you really are?

15

The future – amazing and scary

Coming soon: Amazing –

The Hitchhiker's Guide to the Galaxy

Chapter 1

The house stood on a slight rise just on the edge of the village. It stood on its own and looked out over a broad spread of West Country farmland. Not a remarkable house by any means—it was about thirty years old, squattish, squarish, made of brick, and had four windows set in the front of a size and proportion which more or less exactly failed to please the eye.

The only person for whom the house was in any way special was Arthur Dent, and that was only because it happened to be the one he lived in. He had lived in it for about three years, ever since he had moved out of London because it made him nervous and irritable. He was about thirty as well, tall, darkhaired and never quite at ease with himself. The thing that used to worry him most was the fact that people always used to ask him what he was looking so worried about. He

1%   Locations 72-79   4140

Screens for computers made of electronic paper

You will be able to fold them up and put them in your pocket.

Smart fridges

They work out what you are running out of and order it for you on the Internet.

(Tough if it's something you don't like – it will just keep on arriving!)

Finger phones

Just stick your finger in your ear. (Yes, someone really has invented one.)

I told you you'd like it!

Intelligent spoons

What for? They tell you exactly what you're eating!

SCARY! It will soon be possible to put **tiny microchips** called **RFID** (Radio Frequency Identification) tags into everything you buy.

You won't need to pay for things at the checkout – the tag will automatically send a message to your credit card. If you can't afford it, it won't let you out of the shop!

Sounds great? Yes, but RFIDs can be used to track you wherever you go. They can even be implanted in your body. There's no escape ...

Even scarier! **Spybots** are **tiny aircraft** with **cameras** that can recognise people's faces. Wherever you are, they will find you.

And engineers are working on them now ...

Bludworld3

Chapter 1:
Bludlust the Dragon

Finn approached the cave entrance carefully. There was no sound, but a smell hung in the air – blood!

All around were the bodies of people who had tried their luck – and failed. Two of the burnt bodies were Finn's own.

Finn crept nearer and nearer.

Now the smell of blood changed to a new smell – the stink of dragon!

All was quiet in the cave. The dragon lay sleeping after his last meal of human flesh – one of the bodies that lay scattered round the cave.

Carefully, Finn drew his laser sword from its scabbard.

Then his foot hit a stone. The stone clattered down the cave – and the dragon woke with a roar of fury!

Finn turned to run, but there was no escaping the dragon's breath. Finn felt his clothes burning, then the agony of flames on his back.

Death came quickly ...

Chapter 2:
Another go

Once more, Finn headed into the dragon's cave. His own burnt corpse lay on the floor. That wasn't going to happen this time!

Checking for loose stones, he drew his laser sword from its scabbard.

But there was no dragon.

A young woman, a few years older than Finn, was standing where the dragon usually lay.

She was holding a sheet of paper.

'Who are you? Where's Bludlust?' said Finn.

Then he had a sudden thought.

'I know your game! *You* are the dragon! You've shape-shifted! I've got you now!'

Finn rushed at the woman, and his sword sliced through her neck.

But, for some reason, her head stayed firmly on her body.

Chapter 3:
The Bill

'I'm not a dragon, you idiot!' said the woman, waving the sheet of paper at Finn. 'My name is Misha! Now look at this!'

'What is it?'

'It's your credit card bill!'

Finn took the piece of paper and gasped at it.

'Nearly a million space credits! How am I going to pay for that?

'And how did you know I was here?'

'Your father told me. Finn, you've got to get out of this game! You've been here nearly a week now. The food you're eating isn't real, remember? Your real body is starving to death out there!'

Finn looked puzzled.

'Real body? Oh, of course, I'm playing Bludworld3! It's so real, I forgot who I really am!'

'Well it's a pity your credit card company didn't forget too. These reality games cost a fortune!

'Finn, SNAP OUT OF IT. NOW!'

Chapter 4:
The highest score ever

Finn was eating a huge burger. Misha paid for it – Finn's card was way over the limit.

'Brian – that's the guy who runs the virtual reality world – was getting worried. He thought that you might die for real! He let me into the game to try and talk you out. You would have carried on trying to kill that dragon forever!'

'I'm sorry, Misha. I just love computer games like that. I guess I'm a bit of an addict.'

'Guess so. But Finn, Brian told me something else. He said last week you'd been playing *Galactic Pilot*. He said you got the highest score ever!'

'Guess I'm just a born pilot. On computer games, of course!'

Misha showed Finn a picture of a space ship.

'Do you reckon you could fly one of these – for real?'

'A Q590? Wow! What a dream that would be!'

'It's called the *Lightspinner*, and it's mine. I'm in need of a pilot. If you're up for it, I won't pay you much – but I might just help you with that credit card bill!'

Great Gadgets word check

bombot

body generator

embedded computer

engineer

entertainment

implanted

intelligent

ISP
    (Internet Service
        Provider)

mail server

microchip

prediction

quantum computer

RFID
    (Radio Frequency
        Identification)

spybot

transmitter

virtual world

Answers to the music timeline:

5	Edison cylinder phonograph (1899)
3	Wind-up gramophone (1915)
4	Portable record player (1950s)
7	Sony Walkman cassette player (1980s)
1	Compact disc (CD) player (1995)
2	iPod (2001)
6	Mobile phone (smart phone) (2009)